Traditional Games of Childhood

LET'S PLAY

First U.S. edition 1998

Published in Canada by   Published in U.S. by
Kids Can Press Ltd.   Kids Can Press Ltd.
29 Birch Avenue   85 River Rock Drive, Suite 202
Toronto, ON M4V 1E2   Buffalo, NY 14207

Edited by Trudee Romanek

Printed in Hong Kong
by Wing King Tong Company Limited

US 98 0 9 8 7 6 5 4 3 2 1

Canadian Cataloguing in Publication Data

Gryski, Camilla, 1948–
         Let's play : traditional games of childhood

ISBN 1-55074-497-6

1. Games – Juvenile literature. I. Petričić, Dušan.
II. Title.

GV1203.G79 1998   j796.1'922   C97-931614–6

Traditional Games of Childhood

LET'S PLAY

Illustrated by Dušan Petričić

Written by Camilla Gryski

KIDS CAN PRESS

To my children Miloš, Gordan, Irena and Miša, for keeping me childish. – D. P.

This book is for my friend Caroline, who still knows how to play. – C. G.

I wish to express my warmest thanks to Professor Ivan Ivić
and Danijela Petrović, both from the Institute for Psychology
at Belgrade's Faculty of Philosophy, and to my friend, Zoran Papić,
for their help and support for the idea for this book in its early,
Belgrade phase. – D.P.

I am indebted to the collectors of children's games: Alice Gomme,
William Newell, Jessie Bancroft, Leslie Daiken, Norman Douglas,
Brian Sutton-Smith, Dorothy Howard, Edith Fowke, Iona and Peter
Opie and many others.

My thanks go to the staff of the Osborne Collection of Early
Children's Books, Toronto Public Library, and the staff of the
Museum and Archive of Games at the University of Waterloo. Thank
you also to my family who played with me, to my friends who
helped me remember how we played, and to Dušan for sharing his
idea with me. – C. G.

Pssst! Thank you Trudee.

CONTENTS

INTRODUCTION

People have been playing games for thousands of years. Games have been played in different ways in other times and places, but the patterns are always the same. We love to jump and hop, throw and catch, chase and hide.

Many toys are found in nature. We play with twigs and leaves, pebbles or stones, small bones, nuts and shells.

Other toys are borrowed. Buttons, bottlecaps, rings and thimbles all become part of our games. Games like Tag are played without anything at all.

Most of the games in this book are hundreds of years old. Some games like Jackstones and Hide-and-Seek go back to the ancient Greeks and Romans.

The book tells you how each game can be played, but you and your friends can agree to change the rules. These games belong to you, too. They are yours to play.

COUNTING OUT

There are different ways to choose "It" for games like Tag and Hide-and-Seek. The first one who says "I'm not It" is not It! The last one to reach a tree or a fence has to be It. Or you can choose It by counting out fists, feet or first fingers using a rhyme. Some people think that nonsense counting-out rhymes like "Eeny Meeny Miny Mo" are old ways of counting. Shepherds might have used words like these to count their sheep.

You count out on the beat of the rhyme. If the pointing finger lands on you at the end of the rhyme, you are out.

Two, four, six, eight,
Mary at the garden gate,
Eating cherries off a plate,
Two, four, six, **eight**.

Sky blue, sky blue,
Who's it? Not you!

Engine, engine number nine,
Going down the Chicago line.
If the train falls off the track,
Do you want your money back?
"Yes."
Y-E-S spells yes and
      YOU
      ARE
      NOT
      IT

Put in both fists for:

One potato, two potato,
Three potato, four,
Five potato, six potato,
Seven potato, more.

Mickey Mouse built a house.
How many bricks did he use?
"Four."
1-2-3-4 and out you must go.
Not because you're dirty,
Not because you're clean,
Just because you kissed a girl
Behind a magazine.

The last person left in will be It.

TAG

Chasing and being chased — that's what Tag is all about. In a game of Tag, It can change you with a touch. You might have to freeze until you are freed or hold on to the part of your body that It tagged, while you run. One thing is for sure — you probably won't be It for long!

Puss in the Corner

Puss in the Corner is one of the oldest of all the Tag games. It's for five players.

• Four people make a square, one at each corner. The fifth is in the middle and wants a corner too.

• The people in the corners have to change places. They can call out or signal to the person with whom they want to change. As they change, the person in the middle tries to run to an empty corner.

• The new person without a corner becomes Puss and stands in the middle.

• If Puss is having trouble getting a corner, he can call out "All change." Then all five people scramble for the four corners.

The Moon and the Morning Stars

When the sun shines, you can play the Moon and the Morning Stars.

• The person who is It is the moon. She must stay in the shadow of a building or a large tree.

• The morning stars stay mainly in the sun, but dance in and out of the shadow. Any star who is tagged in the shadow becomes the new moon.

Fox and Geese

Fox and Geese (or Pickadill) is a game for the snow — or the sand.

• In the snow, the players stamp out a large wheel with spokes. There is a safe place at the hub or center of the wheel.

• The fox tries to catch the geese, who run out of the safe center, around the wheel, and across the spokes. The fox must also stay on the paths.

• A goose who is caught changes places with the fox.

Shadow Tag

On a sunny day, try playing Shadow Tag. You are tagged when It steps on your shadow.

Freeze Tag

• When It tags other players, they must freeze on the spot. If a player was standing on one leg with his arms in the air when he was tagged, that's the way he must stay.

• Frozen people can be freed when another player touches them or — and this is harder — if someone crawls between their legs.

• The game ends when everybody is frozen. The last one frozen becomes It for the next game.

PSSST! IN TOUCH TAG, OR STICKY APPLE, YOU MUST HOLD ON TO THE SPOT WHERE YOU WE'RE TAGGED AS YOU RUN. TRY TO TAG PEOPLE IN PLACES THAT MAKE IT HARDER OR FUNNIER FOR THEM TO BE IT, LIKE A KNEE, AN ANKLE OR A NOSE!

13

HIDE-AND-SEEK

All hide and seek games are played in pretty much the same way. Somebody — or a lot of somebodies — is It. Somebody — or a lot of somebodies — hides. There is a safe home base, It has to count before he comes to look, and the hiders have to race to be "home free." Hide-and-Seek has been called "All Hid," "Hideygo," or "Whoop," but it has been played like this for thousands of years.

Here are two ways to play.

Hide-and-Seek

• The person who is It covers her eyes at the spot chosen for home base. She has to count, usually to 50 or 100, while everybody scatters and hides. She shouts "100" or "Ready or not, here I come!" and sets off to search for the hiders.

• When she spots one of them, she has to call out his name and they both race toward Home.

• If she beats him Home, touches the base, and cries "One, two, three on _____," he is caught. But if he reaches home base first and calls out "One, two, three for me," or "One, two, three, home free," he is safe.

• A player doesn't have to wait until he is found to race back Home.

• When all the players are found, the first one caught becomes the new It.

Sardines

Sardines is Hide-and-Seek — but backward.

• All the players cover their eyes and count while one person hides.

• Everybody looks for the hider.

• When a seeker finds the hider, he waits until nobody is near, then creeps into the hiding place with him. The seekers slowly disappear, and the hiding spot becomes more and more cramped. That's why this game is called "Sardines" or "Sardines in a Can."

• The game is over when the last seeker finds the sardines. The first seeker to find the hiding place hides to begin a new game.

A long time ago, the hiders used to signal to the seeker that they were ready by calling out "Whoop!" or "Whoop Oh!" When just one person hid, he called "Spy All!" when he was ready.

HUNT THE THIMBLE

In the game of Hide-and-Seek, what is hidden is well out of sight. In Hunt the Thimble games, something small is hidden, but it's right in front of the eyes of the hunters. The trick is to find it.

Here are two different ways to play. In both, the first person to find the thimble hides it the next time.

Here's a tip: Hide your "thimble" near something that is the same color.

Hot Buttered Beans

• The players wait in another room while one person hides the thimble or other small object. It must be in full view.

• She calls out, "Hot buttered beans! Please come to supper."

• As the other players look for the thimble, she lets them know when they are near. They are "cool" or "freezing" when they are far away; as they get closer, they are "warm," "getting warmer," "burning hot!"

• Sometimes, just one person leaves the room while everybody else hides the thimble.

Huckle Buckle Beanstalk

• One person hides the thimble in full view.

• The other players hunt for the thimble as usual. As each one finds it, he quietly says, "Huckle Buckle Beanstalk," and sits down. He doesn't look at the thimble, of course.

• The game goes on until everybody has found the thimble or until the hider says the game is over.

LEAPFROG

Leapfrog is one of many hopping, leaping and jumping games. It can be played by two friends on their way somewhere, or by many friends to warm up on a chilly morning.

The *Little Pretty Pocket Book* was written for children in 1744. Here is its Leapfrog poem:

This stoops down his Head,
Whilst that springs up high;
But then you will find,
He'll stoop by and by.

That's how two friends play Leapfrog. One friend bends over to make a "back," then the other leaps over him. When the leaper bends over, it is the back's turn to jump.

Tips for backs

• You can make a "little back" on your hands and knees. Tuck in your head.

• You make a "low back" by bending over and grabbing your ankles, or by resting your elbows on your knees.

• When you put your hands on your knees, you make a "high back."

• Always tuck your head in, and stand still and solid.

Tips for leapers

• When you jump, put your hands down flat — no knuckles on the back's back.

• Only your hands touch the back as you go over him.

Hop Frog

This is a leap-frogging game in which everybody hops around.

• To turn yourself into a frog, bend over as if you are going to sit down. Now rest your hands on your knees and spring around. See who can hop for the longest time!

Leapfrog

• The players line up. The first person in the line bends over to make a back. The leaper behind him may ask for "low back" or "high back."

• The leaper jumps over the back, goes a few steps ahead, and bends over to make a back.

• The next in line jumps over these two backs one at a time, then bends over to become the third back in the line.

• When the last player in the line has jumped over all the backs, the first one starts again.

Keep the Kettle Boiling

This game is played like ordinary Leapfrog, but the players stand up to become leapers as soon as they have been leapt over. More than one person is jumping at a time, and the leaper immediately has to become a back for the person behind him.

Sending a Letter

This game comes from London, England. It was originally called Sending a Letter to Canada.

• The first player makes a back. The leaper pretends to write on his back, bang on the stamp, and mail the letter up under his jacket. Then he leaps over the back saying, "Sending a letter."

HOPSCOTCH

There are many ways to play hopping games. You can count your hops, or see who can hop the longest or the farthest. You can add a big step after your hop, and then a jump, to play Hop, Step and Jump. When you draw a pattern on the ground to hop through, you're playing Hopscotch, hopping over lines "scotched" or scratched on the ground. Some of the earliest Hopscotch patterns were probably round and looked like labyrinths or mazes.

To play the game

To play Hopscotch, you need chalk to draw your pattern. Sometimes you also need a marker to throw into each square. Hopscotch markers are often called "pucks." People have always used whatever is handy for a marker — a smooth flat stone, an oyster shell, a broken piece of crockery or a shoe-polish can filled with sand or dirt.

• Draw your pattern — it may look like a snake, a snail or an airplane.

Snake Hopscotch

This pattern is just for hopping through — you don't use a marker. Hop from side to side without touching the lines, or hop up one side and down the other.

PSSST! PLAY IT AT THE BEACH. JUST DRAW YOUR PATTERN IN THE SAND.

Round Hopscotch or the Snail

• Hop around the pattern. Keep your balance and try not to step on any lines. When you get to the space in the center, you can rest there on both feet. Now hop back out.

• Each time you hop into the center and out again without stepping on the lines or putting down your other foot, you write your initials in any square. This space is your Home. You may rest in your home space, but all the other players must hop over it.

• Each player has her own rest spaces, so the hopping can get very tricky.

PSSST! THE HOPSCOTCH REST SPACE HAS BEEN CALLED PLUM PUDDING, HOME OR PARADISE.

Airplane Hopscotch

This pattern is much older than airplanes, but it does have wings. If you like, you can put "ears" around squares 1 and 2. When you stand in the ears, it's easier to throw your marker to the squares near the end of the pattern.

• Throw your marker into 1. Hop over 1, into 2 and then 3. Land in 4 and 5, one foot in each. Hop into 6 and land in 7 and 8 together. Square 9 is a hop, and 10 is a turn-around rest space. Land in it on two feet, turn around with a jump, then start hopping back.

• Hop all the way back to 2, bend over, pick up your marker, and hop into 1 and out of the pattern.

• The marker must always land inside the lines of each space. Don't step on any lines, and try not to fall over.

• Throw your marker into 2. Hop into 1, over 2 and keep going, hopping and landing through the pattern to the end. Turn around, hop back to 3, pick up your marker from 2, hop through 2 and 1, and out of the pattern. When your marker is in one of the landing spaces – 4 or 5, 7 or 8 – you won't be able to land on two feet: you'll have to hop through that part of the pattern.

• When you've thrown your marker to 9 (you can use the ears) and hopped all the way there to get it and then back, the game is over.

• If you are taking turns to play, you start your next turn where you stopped the last time.

Try playing the game these ways:

• Throw your marker into 1, and hop into 1 after it. Now, with your hopping foot, kick the marker into 2, then 3. You hop and kick with the same foot, so you shuffle the marker to the end of the pattern and back. You can hop and shuffle more than once in each square, but neither you nor your marker may land on any lines.

• Hop through the pattern balancing your marker on your hand, your elbow or the top of your head.

HOPSCOTCH

JUMPING ROPE

Spring is jumping rope season. People used to think that jumping around in the spring would make the crops grow. They hoped that the plants would grow as high as the jumpers jumped. When jumping rope first became popular, it was a boy's game. Boys did tricks like turning the rope twice for one jump and jumping with crossed hands. Later, girls added the rhymes.

You can skip alone, holding the ends of a short rope. When you skip with your friends using a long rope, the people turning the rope are called "enders."

Skippers usually run in and out of the rope, but you can also stand in and start on the count of three.

Ipsey, Pipsey,
Tell me true,
Who shall I be married to?
A ... B ... C ... D ...

(Skip rope until you trip on a letter. It's the first letter of your future sweetheart's name!)

Jumping rope has its own language.

Salt *(Turn the rope slowly.)*

Mustard and Vinegar *(Turn the rope at normal speed.)*

Pepper or Peppers *(This has always meant turning the rope as quickly as you can.)*

Bluebells *(The rope swings from side to side. It doesn't go over the skipper's head. This is also called Rocking the Cradle.)*

High water *(The rope doesn't touch the ground as it turns.)*

Chase the fox *(All the players follow the fox, doing what she does as she runs under the rope or skips once or twice.)*

Under the moon *(The skippers run under the rope, without skipping.)*

Over the stars *(The skippers jump once over the rope.)*

House to rent,
Enquire within.
When I jump out,
Let _____ jump in.

(This is one of the oldest jump rope rhymes. Call in a friend, jump a couple of times together, then jump out. Your friend stays in to call a new friend.)

Bluebells, cockleshells,
Eevy, ivy, over.
My mother sent me to the store,
And this is what she sent me for:
Salt, mustard, vinegar, pepper!

(For "pepper," the enders turn the rope as fast as they can.)

Grapes on the vine,
Ready to be picked.
One fell off,
And the other did the splits.

(Skip until "splits," then stop the rope between your legs.)

Apples, peaches, pears and plums,
Tell me when your birthday comes.
January, February, March ...
First, second, third ...

(Jump in on your birthday month, and jump out on the date.)

PSSST! TRY PEELING THE APPLE. JUMP IN. JUMP ALL AROUND THE PERSON WHO IS SKIPPING. THE "APPLE," THE PEELED APPLE RUNS OUT AND YOU STAY IN TO BE PEELED.

BALLS

Balls may be the oldest toys. People rolled, or threw and caught, anything that was round. Later on, balls were made of strips of leather sewn together and stuffed with hair or feathers. The first ball games were games of catch, but bouncy balls and paved school yards changed the way people play with balls.

Queenie

• The player chosen to be Queenie stands with her back to the other players and throws a ball backward over her head. The other players all try to catch it. When one has it, the players put their hands behind their backs.

• Queenie turns around and guesses who has the ball. If she is right, she is Queenie again. If she is wrong, the person who has the ball becomes Queenie.

Call Ball

You can play this game by throwing the ball into the air or by bouncing it high against a wall.

• Each player is given a number or the name of one of the days of the week.

• The first player throws the ball and calls out a day or a number.

• The player whose day or number is called has to run and catch the ball before it bounces more than once.

• If he catches the ball, he calls next. If he misses, the first player throws and calls again.

Four Square

This is a game for four players and a line of people waiting for a turn. Use a rubber ball you can bounce with two hands.

• Draw a big square on the ground and divide it up into four smaller squares. Each person stands in a small square.

• Choose a subject: colors, animals, names of boys or girls, states or movies.

• The player with the ball calls out a color, for example, or a name, and bounces the ball into any other square.

• The person standing in that square catches the ball, then does the same. The ball bounces from square to square. The players may not repeat any words.

• If someone misses a catch or can't think of a word, the next player waiting in line steps into his square. The new player can dash in to try to keep the game going, or the players can choose to start a new game with a new category.

Ball bouncing

Rhymes are used for ball bouncing, skipping and clapping — you can bounce your ball instead of clapping, or skip to a ball-bouncing chant. Here are two games to try.

O'Leary is a ball-bouncing game. Bounce the ball for "One, two, three." Your leg goes over the bouncing ball each time you say "O'Leary." Catch the ball at the end.

One, two, three, O'Leary,
Four, five, six, O'Leary,
Seven, eight, nine, O'Leary,
Ten, O'Leary,
Catch me.

Ordinary Moving is a wall-ball game. You throw the ball against the wall, then do something before you catch it. Or you might have to catch the ball in a certain way. You can let the ball bounce once. Chant the words as you throw and catch.

Ordinary (*Throw the ball and catch it.*)

Moving (*Throw the ball and catch it without moving your feet.*)

Laughing (*Throw and catch the ball. Keep a straight face.*)

Talking (*Throw the ball, touch your mouth, then catch the ball.*)

One hand (*Throw and catch with one hand.*)

The other hand (*Throw and catch with the other hand.*)

One foot (*Throw and catch while standing on one foot.*)

The other foot (*Throw and catch while standing on the other foot.*)

Clap front (*Throw, clap your hands, and catch the ball.*)

Clap back (*Throw, clap behind your back, and catch the ball.*)

Front and back (*Throw, clap in front, then behind your back, and catch the ball.*)

Back and front (*Throw, clap behind your back, then in front, and catch the ball.*)

Tweedles (*Throw, twirl your hands around each other one way, and catch the ball.*)

Twidles (*Throw, twirl your hands around each other the other way, and catch the ball.*)

And away she goes (*Throw, spin around, and catch the ball.*)

If you can do all this without dropping the ball, try going through the whole chant throwing and catching the ball without moving. (*When you come to "One foot" and "The other foot" just touch them. And wave your arms around for "Away she goes."*) Then you can try keeping a straight face through the whole chant, or touching your mouth, and so on. You could be busy all day!

PSSST! TRY BOUNCING YOUR BALL TO ONE, TWO, BUCKLE MY SHOE.

28

CLAPPING GAMES

"Peas Porridge Hot" was one of the first clapping rhymes. People used it on wintery mornings to warm up their hands. Perhaps that's why one of the names for this game is Hot Hands. It's easy to get mixed up, and you have to think hard to keep up with your partner. But the faster you play, the better.

There are lots of ways to clap. Here are some of them.

- Clap your hands on your legs.
- Clap your own hands together.
- Clap your friend's hands:

Clap both hands straight on, nothing fancy.

You and your friend clap right hands, clap your own hands, then clap left hands.

You and your friend clap the backs of each other's hands, turn your hands, then clap straight on.

Turn your hands so that one palm faces up toward the sky and one faces down toward the ground. Your friend does the same. Your sky hand claps her ground hand, and your ground hand claps her sky hand. Now flip each hand over and do it again.

- Cross your hands on your chest between claps.

Start with this clap for "Peas Porridge Hot." Clap the same pattern for each line.

Peas porridge hot,

(Clap your hands on your legs, clap your own hands, clap your friend's hands.)

Peas porridge cold,
Peas porridge in the pot,
Nine days old.
Some like it hot,
Some like it cold,
Some like it in the pot,
Nine days old.

PSSST! YOU CAN CLAP TO ANYTHING. TRY OTHER NURSERY RHYMES, ADVERTISEMENTS, YOUR FAVORITE SONG OR A WORD LIKE MISSISSIPPI!

Use this longer clapping pattern for each line of "A Sailor Went to Sea."

A sailor went to sea, sea, sea,

(Clap your own hands, clap right hands, clap your own hands, clap left hands, clap your own hands, clap straight on three times.)

To see what he could see, see, see,
But all that he could see, see, see,
Was the bottom of the deep blue
  sea, sea, sea.

Follow the clapping pattern through "When Johnny Was One."

When Johnny was one,
He learned to suck his thumb,

(Clap own hands, clap straight on, clap own hands, clap right hands, clap own hands, clap left hands, clap own hands, clap straight on.)

(Clap own hands.)

Thumbdoodle, thumbdoodle,

(Clap right hands, clap own hands, clap left hands, clap own hands)

Half past one.

(Cross hands on chest, clap on legs, clap straight on.)

When Johnny was two,
He learned to tie his shoe,
Thumbdoodle, thumbdoodle,
Half past two.

When Johnny was three,
He learned to climb a tree.

... four, he learned to shut the door.

... five, he learned to take a dive.

... six, he learned to pick up sticks.

... seven, he learned to go to heaven.

... eight, he learned to shut the gate.

... nine, he learned to tell the time.

... ten, he learned to feed the hens.

When Johnny was ... Goodbye!

HAND GAMES

Flashing Fingers was played in Egypt four thousand years ago and it's still being played today. Whether you're playing a game with hand shapes, making a tall pile of hands, or wiggle-waggling your thumbs, your hands are the "handiest" toys.

Hands on Hands

This game is fun to play with lots of people.

• Gather around a table or other flat surface for the game. The first player puts his hand on the table with the palm facing down. Now each player in turn adds one hand to the stack. When each player has put in one hand, the players go around the circle again. This time each player puts in his other hand.

• When the pile is finished, the players pull their hands out, one by one, from the bottom of the pile and put them on top of the stack.

Flashing Fingers

Here's how to "flash" your fingers. Shake your closed hand twice, then flash out your fingers on the count of three.

There are different ways to play this game.

• One player flashes out a number of fingers on one hand, and the other player guesses how many. The finger flasher and the guesser both use the three count. They must flash and guess at exactly the same time.

• Two players flash fingers on the count of three. At the same time, each player calls out the number of fingers she thinks the other player will flash.

• Two players play together. Each one flashes fingers and calls out her guess for *all* the fingers flashed. Each player must decide how many fingers she will flash (from one to five), guess how many her friend will flash (from one to five), and then figure out what the total will be.

PSSST! SCISSORS, PAPER, STONE CAN ALSO BE USED TO CHOOSE IT.

Scissors, Paper, Stone

In this game, you flash hand shapes. In each pair of shapes there is a winner.

- Make scissors with your index and middle fingers.
- Paper is a flat hand, palm facing down.
- Stone is a closed fist.

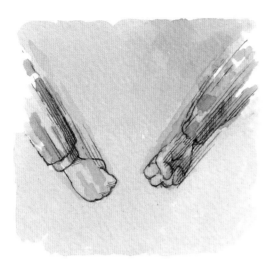

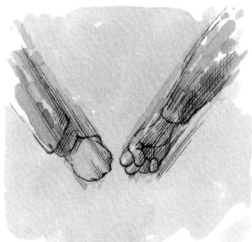

- Scissors cut paper, so they win.

- Paper covers stone, so it wins.

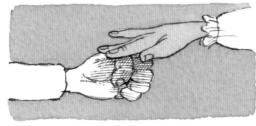

- Stone can smash scissors, so it wins.

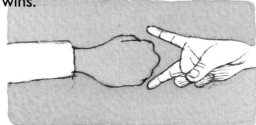

If you both flash the same shape, try again.

Wiggle-Waggle

Wiggle-Waggle is Simon Says with thumbs.

- To play, make your hands into fists and stick your thumbs out.
- When Simon calls "Simon says thumbs up," stick your thumbs up.
- When Simon says thumbs down, turn your hands so that your thumbs point down.
- When Simon says Wiggle-waggle, wiggle your thumbs.
- Don't do any of these unless "Simon says ..."

HAND SHADOWS

Shadows on the wall — funny, spooky or beautiful. They're magical because they look so different from the hands that make them.

Here are some tips for shadow makers.

• Use a small light source like a reading lamp or a flashlight. The light bulb should be clear, not frosty. Frosty bulbs are for people who don't want shadows.

• For a screen, use a bare wall that's a light color, or tape up a piece of white paper.

• Sit or stand between the light and the wall. The light, you, and the screen must be in a straight line.

• Move yourself or move the light until you get dark shadows with clear outlines.

• Don't look at your hands, look at the shadows you are making.

Now try making some shadow pictures.

Duck

Elephant

Cow

Bird

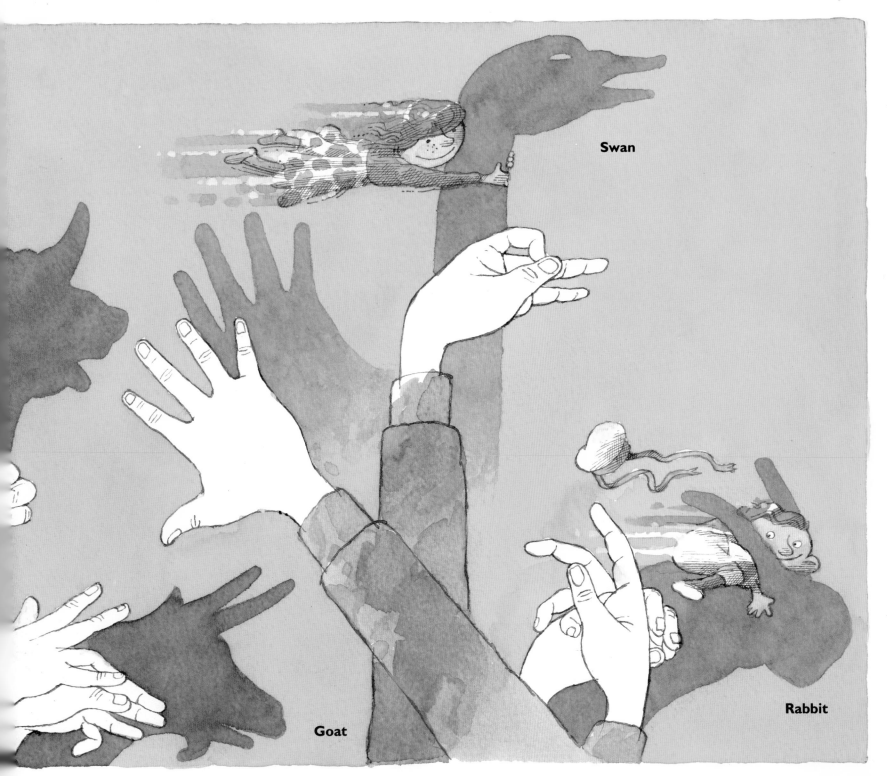

Swan

Goat

Rabbit

TELEPHONE

If you had played this game a hundred years ago, you would have called it Russian Scandal. Now we call it Gossip, Telephone or Broken Telephone.

It's easy to play. All you need is a group of friends with ears!

- The players sit in a circle or a row.

- The first player whispers something, just once, to his neighbor — a phrase or a sentence.

- The neighbor whispers what she heard — or thinks she heard — to the person next to her.

- The message is passed on from player to player. The last person to hear the message repeats it out loud. The message will get funnier and odder as it is passed along.

JACKSTONES

In ancient Greece and Rome, this game was called Astragals because it was played with the astragalus or ankle bone of a sheep. Players threw five "knucklebones" up into the air and tried to catch them on the backs of their hands. The same throwing and catching game is played with five stones, five shells, little silk beanbags filled with rice, or jacks and a ball.

Jacks

Jacks are small metal shapes that are used instead of real knucklebones. They are easy to pick up because they sit on only three of their six legs. The game is played with five or ten of these jacks and a small rubber ball.

You can throw the ball up and let it bounce once before you catch it, or you can bounce it down, let it bounce up, and then catch it. See which way you like best.

Here are some ways to play with five jacks and a ball.

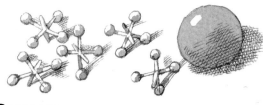

Scatters

• Scatter your jacks on the ground.

• Onesies: Throw the ball, pick up one jack, then catch the ball with the same hand. Put the jack in your other hand. Throw the ball again and pick up the next jack, then catch the ball. Do this until you have picked up all the jacks one by one.

• Twosies: This time you pick up the jacks two at a time. Look at the scattered jacks and choose carefully which two you will scoop up together each time. If you are just starting, "Dubs" might be allowed — you may arrange the jacks before you try to pick them up.

Throw the ball, pick up two jacks, catch the ball. Put the jacks in your other hand. Throw the ball and pick up two more jacks, then catch the ball. Put these two jacks into your other hand as well. Throw the ball, pick up the last jack, then catch the ball.

• Threesies: Pick up three jacks on your first throw, then two on your second. Now it's even more important to choose which jacks you will scoop up together each time.

- Foursies: Throw the ball, scoop up four jacks, then catch the ball. Pick up the last jack on your next throw.

- Fivesies: Scatter the jacks, but not too far apart. Throw the ball and scoop up all the jacks before you catch it.

PSSST! WITH STONES, THREESIES IS ALSO CALLED THE HORSE AND CART. THE THREE STONES ARE THE CART. THE SINGLE STONE IS THE HORSE.

Fivestones

Scatters can be played without a ball and with stones instead of jacks. Fivestones is a much faster game than Jacks. A bouncing ball gives you more time to pick up your playing pieces than a falling stone does.

You can collect some smooth pebbles to use for this game. They should be round enough to be picked up easily, but not so round that they roll away. Keep looking until you have five special pebbles to keep in your pocket.

Once you have scattered your stones, choose one to throw — it's called your "sky stone." Toss up your sky stone, scoop up a stone from the ground, and catch the sky stone in the same hand. Put the stone in your other hand. Pick up all the stones one by one this way.

Work your way through Twosies, Threesies and Foursies just as you would with jacks and a ball. For each round, choose your sky stone carefully so that the ones you leave are the easiest to pick up together. After Foursies, all five stones are in your hand ready to go back into your pocket.

Pigs in the Pen

This jacks game is also called Cherries in the Basket. You can play it with five stones if you like.

- Scatter the jacks.

- Make a pigpen by resting the side of your hand on the ground and curving your fingers and thumb to make an opening.

- Throw the ball and push one of the "pigs" into the pigpen. Catch the ball. One by one, push all the other pigs into the pen. You can try pushing them into the pen two by two as well.

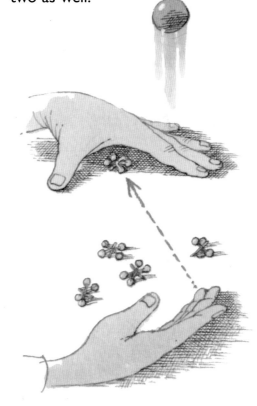

Horses in the Stable

You can play this game with jacks and a ball or with five stones.

• Make a stable for your "horses" by spreading out your fingers and thumb, and resting your fingertips on the ground.

• Put one jack into each of the four "doorways." The jacks stay near the tips of your fingers and thumb.

• Throw the ball and push one of the horses into the stable. Keep throwing the ball and pushing the horses into the stable one by one until all four jacks are inside your hand.

• Throw the ball one last time and scoop up all four horses.

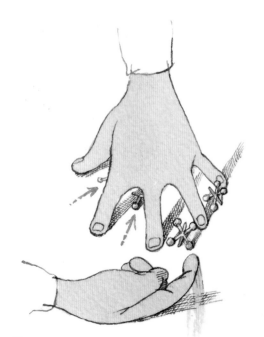

Sweep the Floor

This is a game for five stones, but you can use jacks and a ball.

• Scatter the stones.

• Throw the sky stone and, with your fingertips, sweep one of the stones nearer to the others. Catch the sky stone.

• Throw the sky stone again and use your fingertips to sweep another stone closer to the others. Catch the stone. Do this until you have swept all the stones together.

• Throw the sky stone one more time and pick up all the other stones.

PSSST! TRY PEACH PITS.

Danger

Here's one last game. It's for stones or jacks without the ball, and it's difficult — so it's a game to practice carefully. See how far you can get.

• Scatter your stones.

• Throw your sky stone and scoop up one stone. Catch your sky stone. Now there are two stones in your hand.

• Throw two stones, scoop up a stone from the ground, and catch the two stones as they fall. Now you have three stones in your hand.

• Try to throw three stones, scoop up the fourth, and catch the three. If you line up the three stones along the palm of your hand before you throw them, they have a better chance of falling down together.

• The game ends when you manage to throw up four stones, scoop up the last stone, and end with five stones in your hand.

MARBLES

Marrididdles, cat's eyes and taws — marbles have their own language. Marrididdles are homemade marbles made of clay and left to dry in the sun. Cat's eyes are glass marbles with swirls of color inside. And a taw? That's another name for the favorite marble with which you shoot.

Long before there were marbles, people rolled smooth pebbles or built little pyramids of nuts and tried to knock them down. Early marbles were made of stone or clay, but they've also been made of wood, steel, agate and other semi-precious stones, and glass. Looking at the patterns inside the little glass balls is one of the delights of marbles.

But marbles are to be played with, not just looked at. You can choose to play for fun — you get your marbles back at the end of the game — or for keeps. You and your friends should agree which way to play before you begin the game.

You can roll, toss or shoot a marble.

To shoot a marble

• Curl your fingers. Put your thumb nail behind your index finger. Practice flicking it forward, out from behind your index finger. It's that flick that shoots the marble.

• Rest the marble in the little space made by your curled index finger and your thumb. You can curl your index finger a little more to hold the marble there.

• Now "knuckle down" – rest the knuckle of your index finger on the ground. Flick your thumb and send your marble flying along the ground.

Hits and Spans

You and a friend can play this marble chase game when you are going somewhere together.

• The first player shoots her marble.

• The second player shoots her marble, trying to hit the first marble or to come within a span of it. (You "span" two marbles by spreading out your index finger and thumb. You should be able to touch both marbles at the same time.) If she does, she wins the marble. If she doesn't, she leaves her marble there and her friend has a chance to shoot at it.

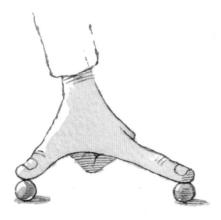

• The winner — the person who hits or spans her friend's marble — starts the game again. Of course, you could use the same two marbles over and over.

Plum Pudding or Picking Plums

• Each player puts a number of marbles on a line.

• The players take turns shooting at the marbles. A player wins the ones he knocks off the line. If he misses, he has to wait his turn to play again.

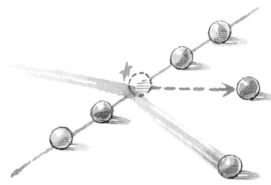

The Ring Game

Draw a ring on the ground or use a ring you find lying around, like a circular pattern in the carpet.

• Each player puts a number of marbles into the ring.

• The players agree to a starting line a little distance away from the ring. To see who will go first, each player shoots a marble from the starting line toward the ring. The player whose marble is closest to the ring will shoot first, followed by the player whose marble is the next closest. The players pick up their marbles to use as shooters for the game.

• To begin the game, the first player knuckles down at the starting line and shoots, trying to hit a marble out of the ring.

• If a player knocks a marble out of the ring and his shooter goes out too, he gets to keep the marble and he takes another turn. This time he shoots from where his shooter lies.

• If a player knocks a marble out of the ring but his shooter is left inside, he can get it back by putting a marble into the ring in its place. He is out of the game and must put the marbles he has won back into the ring.

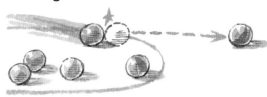

• If a player misses and his shooter stays inside the ring, he can put a marble into the ring to get it back. He is out until the next game.

• If a player misses and his shooter rolls outside the ring, it stays there until his next turn. Then he will shoot from where his shooter lies.

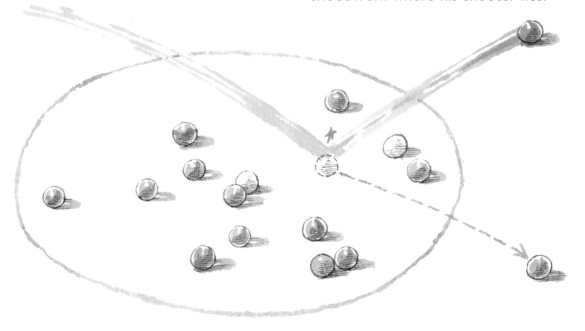

MARBLES

PSSST!
TRY THIS GAME:
THE PLAYERS SHOOT
THEIR MARBLES
AT A WALL.
THE PLAYER WHOSE
MARBLE IS THE CLOSEST
TO THE WALL
WINS ALL THE
MARBLES.

The artwork in this book was rendered in watercolor and pen and ink on 140 lb
Bockingford watercolor paper.

Text is set in Gill Sans
Hand lettering done by the artist

Printed in Hong Kong by Wing King Tong Company Limited